PRAISE FOR A FLAG OF NO NATION

"Inspired by his ancestral story of Sephardi diasporas across empires and nation-states, Haviv has produced a moving and visionary critique of the intractable Israeli/Palestinian conflict. *A Flag of No Nation* moves from the phantasmagoric to the concrete, from the disturbing blindness of nationalisms to new visions of peace. He makes powerful use of voice, not only through his poetic imagination but also through oral history, in recorded conversations with his grandmother, documented in time and beautifully phrased in verse. He reminds us of the importance of history and family memory in envisioning a different pathway toward inclusivity and equality."

—Rina Benmayor, professor emerita at California State University, Monterey Bay and author of *Romances judeo-españoles de Oriente* (Eastern Judeo-Spanish Ballads)

"Like the 'confident acrobat' he has so gently envisioned, Tom Haviv's beautiful poetry and art ripple through the pages of this book, opening doors where surprises smile all of a sudden, connecting the most daunting dots of our yearnings. What's the reason for a flag? To whom belongs this poem? Traveling through imagined landscapes and inherited narratives of loss, Haviv creates a home here, perhaps even a sacred temporary haven, a place for us to land."

—Rabbi Amichai Lau-Lavie, founder of Lab/Shul

"The son of an Israeli fighter pilot, and the grandson of activists with Istanbul's underground Zionist youth movement, Haviv is all too aware that the story — like matter — cannot be destroyed, only refashioned. Using a number of different modes — from allegory to oral history to the lyric poem — Haviv attempts to chart a path through the collective making and unmaking of the Zionist narrative to a proposed remaking in a post-Zionist context, declaring that path as valid and as rooted as the one that created and sustained the original Zionist myth. What Haviv has given us in *A Flag of No Nation* is a map of this almost alchemical process, a necessary one if we're ever to break through to something new."

—Arielle Angel, editor of *Jewish Currents*

"I was captivated from the first paragraph of Tom Haviv's book when he witnesses his storytelling accomplice, transhistorical spirit guide, subject, and grandmother Yvette pour deep time into her waiter's ear. Huge gratitude to both of them for providing an experience full of geographical landings and historical surfaces where our thoughts and feelings can rest while they share their minutely observant journey through Jewish and Levantine identity in the 20th century. It is truly wonderful when a prismatic work of art girds the reader for strategic action in real life. Thank you Tom and Yvette."

—Jenny Romaine, theater artist and organizer

"Tom Haviv's *A Flag of No Nation* is a magnificent rendering of family history and migration, as presented through 'this cascade of choices/we call our stories.' Dedicated to his grandmother Yvette, Haviv's meditative and visionary book of poems gathers and disperses the ephemera of the past in a structurally inventive and fluid landscape of text, image, pixels, and sound. The reader, set on a voyage at once mythical and digital, is dazzled by Haviv's explorations of style and the concert of voices that guide the multitudinous sections of this book. *A Flag of No Nation* recalls and reveres generations in a compassionate timescape that yields, like land appearing on the horizon, something sublime and unknown."

—Connie Mae Concepción Oliver, author of *science fiction fiction* and editor of *FEELINGS*

"*A Flag of No Nation* is an artful and tragic, ambitious and generous book. Its enveloping intimacy humbles us as much as it estranges, inviting us to imagine those political possibilities weaving together beneath our very noses."

—Ben Ratskoff, founder and editor-in-chief of *PROTOCOLS*

"*A Flag of No Nation* is as much architecture as it is verse. Haviv's poems build up and down the page, like houses being constructed — or perhaps demolished. They invite you in, to learn distractedly. Not as from a litany or a liturgy but wandering and inhabiting a broken library with fragments of different worlds and times, the recent history of the near east, family, migration, and oh so many breaks. He has, in his own way, politicized aesthetics. Not in the trivial way that the poems are about politics — although so many, if certainly not all, are. But in the way that the poetry works on you, pushes and pulls you, stretches where your senses might end. It asks you questions. Not directly. And I suppose not one question — it asks you about memory and time and history, how to record a string of events, why to make a flag, where family stories end and official stories begin. It asks you to ask questions. The poems make demands on you. And the question cannot just linger — you can't get away that easy once you've walked inside."

—Ajay Singh Chaudhary, executive director of the Brooklyn Institute for Social Research

"Tom Haviv's *A Flag of No Nation* is an interdisciplinary amalgam of poetic forms — myth, oral family history, political ethnography, conceptual performance art, and imagistic alchemy. Each chapter follows a different aesthetic path to the same critical point: the intersection of history with the human heart. By artfully weaving together the living memories of his own family members as they sought to navigate a monumentally volatile moment in Ottoman, European, Jewish, and Palestinian history, Haviv never lets the reader collapse the multidimensionality of life or the complexities of our various identities, both inherited and constructed, into rigidified theory. We have heard the truism for decades that 'the personal is political,' and Haviv's genre-bending work of poetic activism creatively and compassionately reminds us all of the more complex and messier truth that the political is also personal. This is a daring new work of political imagination that is inspiringly ambitious in scope, while at the same time accessible and enjoyable to read and discuss."

—Eden Pearlstein (ePRHYME), multimedia artist and educator

"Tom Haviv takes the beauty, pain, and particularity of his family's immigration stories and examines them like a precious stone, with each side and angle revealing a different depth of identity, history, contemporary relevance, and questioning. At once sweeping and intimate, Haviv's words and images linger with vivid color and brilliant sensation on every page, as the poems mingle characters, flags and journeys, chronologies and deep loves between people. Haviv's work is political as he sensitively brings out a complex allegory at the precise moment when understanding intersectional identities and reimagining togetherness may be the only things that can truly save us."

—Libby Lenkinski, vice president for public engagement at the New Israel Fund

A FLAG OF NO NATION

Poems

Tom Haviv

A Flag of No Nation
By Tom Haviv

This book was made possible with the generous support of Anne Germanacos. We are grateful for her commitment to the transformative power of creative work, and to amplifying a polyphony of voices from within and beyond the Jewish world.

Second Edition
First Printing

Cover design, book design, and typesetting by
Lucy Andersen & Tom Haviv

Ayin Press
Brooklyn, New York
www.ayinpress.org
info@ayinpress.org

Distributed by Publishers Group West, an Ingram brand
Printed in China

ISBN (paperback): 978-1-961814-05-9
ISBN (e-book): 978-1-961814-06-6

Library of Congress Control Number: 2024930245

Ayin Press books may be purchased at a discounted rate by wholesalers, booksellers, book clubs, schools, universities, synagogues, community organizations, and other institutions buying in bulk. For more information, please email info@ayinpress.org.

Follow us on Facebook, Instagram, or Twitter @AyinPress.

A Flag of No Nation was previously published by Jewish Currents Press. Gratitude to the whole team at Jewish Currents, and to Ari Bloomekatz for his support on the first edition.

dağ dağa kavuşmaz, insan insana kavuşur

although mountain does not meet mountain, man can meet man

TABLE OF CONTENTS

"Where are you from?"
the waitress asked my grandmother
after hearing the lilt of her accent.

"Córdoba,"
my grandmother replied in a breath
as if speaking on a stage to thousands.

My grandmother Yvette was born in 1928 in Istanbul to a Sephardi Jewish family. Her relatives were from Izmir, Salonika, Adana, Athens, and Mersin. In 1949, she and my grandfather moved to Israel where they would live together for 60 years. That day, however, in a cafe in rural Ohio, she said "Córdoba," the city of her ancestors, Jews who had fled the Inquisition in the 15th century. Córdoba: *an unbreakable story.*

A Flag of No Nation is my offering to a history that is only beginning to be written: the story of Turkish Jews in the 20th century. It is fundamentally a work of mythmaking: of family folklore, of allegory, of visions of a world to come.

This book is designed to be an instrument of dreaming and action; a talisman that helps its readers pass through barriers of time, language, and distance — through the walls of the political present — and further, beyond the walls of political imagination.

Throughout the book, the reader will find Yvette's stories and poetry guiding us through her life, across oceans of time and memory. Over five years, I recorded our conversations in audio and video, and archived all of our emails. I present here her voice, word by word, changing only a few details for readability. The primary intervention is the line break: the shifting shore of text and absence, the trace of my listening, of my appreciation of her words and her voice.

The book begins in allegory (Island), turns to oral history (Losslessness) and then to lyric document (Ladder | Allegiance and An Arrow A Wing), and closes with performance texts (A Flag of No Nation) and political visions (Hamsa Flag).

this book is written for my grandmother Yvette (1928–2019)
may her memory be a blessing

ISLAND

14

I
OCEAN

A line of silent marks on an expanse of white.

Tightly packed ships drifting into white ocean,
travelers singing of a white sun,

white light falling evenly overhead;
no sign of land, no trace of wind.

Night and day reel;
a golden year passes:
the travelers are lost.

A blue-eyed man tosses his oar into the sea.
With a free hand, he reaches for his right eye, takes it out, tosses it ahead of him.
As soon as the eye falls in, a rock breaks through the water's surface.

II
ISLAND

The travelers in the nearby ships gasp, leap to their feet, lean over their bows to watch in wonder
as more and more objects burst through the surf:
jagged outlooks, cliffs, soft heaving mosses . . .

The blue-eyed man doesn't waver; his ship and its passengers drift ahead, as an entire island forms behind.
With his other hand, he reaches for his left eye, removes it, tosses it ahead of him, as far as he can
into white ocean.

Another rock bursts out of the water; wake forms.
The travelers hold onto their vessels tightly, as two landmasses emerge: small, naked, black and brown rocks jutting into open air.
One by one, against the wake, the travelers stand, as if in salute, and pluck out their eyes, throwing them as far as they can into the white ocean.
Some groan in pain, others in relief; all hands coated red.

The rocks' peaks push higher and higher, splaying water, producing more wake.
The travelers, the men & the women, empty out their sockets: a rain, a volley of eyes, stratifying the white sky.
Islands burst into view wherever an eye sinks
until nearly all the travelers go blind.

The children look on in shock.
The eldest, without much thought, in a show of bravery even, follow suit, imitate their elders, and empty their sight.
The youngest, those who were born at sea, without a memory of home, Rimona, cannot.
The very sight (the blood, what had formed) is frightening; few have the courage to watch, let alone imitate what they see.
So the youngest keep their eyes.
And together, the blind & the youngest grip their vessels, as they watch an entire archipelago dry.

III
LANDING

The blue-eyed man, with the confidence of an acrobat, steps off the boat, wading through shallow water, to meet a land flowering softly beneath his feet.
From the shore, he calls out the need to build the bare necessities.
He sings the contents of everything he can imagine, everything he can remember from home, from books: fires, tools, encampments . . .
But without sight, he can only stand for so long on the slippery shore. Before even taking a second step,
he falls on all fours and is forced to feel with his hands and knees.
He keeps crawling further onto the island. He does so since it is easier and, he also reasons, in order to feel more.
As he crawls — and as the earth below him greens — he grows confident in the image of the world that he wants to have built.

Homes, homes, homes, he sings.
The elders, the men & the women, follow the first man, whose name was America, onto the landmass he has chosen, the largest island that formed.
They crawl out of the ships, slipping on rocks, which were quietly gaining the friction of grass and dirt.
Yet when they stand, they wobble, and fall to the ground, and begin to crawl too:
even the fresh green is too tender to stand on.
When they finally set foot on the earth, they feel something like joy and relief;
when good things arrive by accident: that is, without work.
The adults crawl faster and grasp the earth: sands, small trees, soft rodents, and white light, its heat pressing on their backs.
It occurs to them, and soon to their children, who had been called to witness the land, that, due to endless days and nights at sea,
the travelers had not built anything in many years.
So a woman calls out to the youngest children,
What can you see? Can you tell us what you see?

The children see a place well-nourished, full-of-image, but without-human.
The ocean had been without-image.
What they see before them now is a place they could truly read, sing. The woman asks, more insistently,
What can you see? Can you tell us what you see?
What do you think we can build here?
The children quietly take in their surroundings . . .
They feel the heft of what had not yet been described.
They reflect on what had been said. They breathe.
As soon as the first child speaks, they know they have signed onto a tight covenant:
they have been enslaved by their parents, enslaved by the need to tell,
to recount, to record, to catalogue.
Enslaved by the need to describe.

IV
WHAT THE EARTH SAW

An elder called out, leapt to his feet.
(The elders had been resting, reclining, basking under the slim shade of newly formed trees,
some of which were still accelerating into native height before the children's eyes.
The youngest stood above them.
They were the same height as the adults when they were on all fours.
Some of them, feeling playful in their new responsibility, would ride on the backs of their blind parents.)
An elder raised his arms wildly and yelled,
The earth! It saw us! We let it see us!
People woke from rest. *The earth saw us,* many stood up to say, as if in clear agreement.
They screamed and hummed it, sang and laughed it.
The earth, an eye, watched us while we were vulnerable on all fours, one man reasoned.

They felt shame, like a refrain of a work song for those who had never worked.
They sang, *the earth / it saw us / we let it see us.*
In fear of ridicule from an earth that could see, they covered their palms and feet.
Shoes from their own skin at first, excess from calves and backs, then later
vellum from small grazing animals, their fingers red, or the pale green of leaves.
The earth saw us, a blind man said, mostly to himself, mumbling, but also to his children.
Then he said more audibly, *The earth looked on, since we landed . . .*
And he turned to the children (bringing everyone's attention with him) and began to describe his vision for the flow of description,
an industry even: how it would be siphoned, consumed,
processed by the reclining adults, a feedback loop to create their new colony.
Yet the children were not afraid; they were in awe of that which was in front of them.
The island fully green. Lush. Calls of birds. A clearing. A sign: the world could be made again.

A woman whispered insistently to the children,
What can you see? Can you tell us what you see?
And the children began to sing *The Myth of Obstacle.*

THE MYTH OF OBSTACLE

There's a door in the water
A door in the air
A well in a tree
A window in the earth.

A door in the word
A door in the hour
A door in the mirror
A door in the air
A door in the year
A door in the wall
A door in the earth
A door in the ear . . .

A well in the word
A well in the hour
A well in the door
A well in the year
A well in the air
A well in the wall
A well in the tree
A well in the ear . . .

A window in the word
A window in the water
A window in the hour
A window in the mirror
A window in the air
A window in the year
A window in the hand
A window in the ear . . .

After the shore
The song begins
White not abstract
silent

After the shore
of empire
After empire
After the song of empire
After the song of sense
After the song of
After the shore of
After the song of
After the shore of the song
After the shore of the song of the shore of the song

V
PYRAMIDS OF SOUND

As they sang (of window, water, well) they articulated a space: a thinly wooded slope leading to a clearing, where they found a river.
Sounds thickened:
branches against branches, animals (turtles, rodents, snakes, finches, hawks), slow sands, whistling caves, a warm breeze through a field.
Yet high over all, the noise of children's descriptions reigned. Their voices rumbled, constantly recording.
As the blind parents, reclining, received the descriptions, the island began to hold a stiller and stiller shape in their minds.

*

Sometimes, like the last spasm of a dying body, an image of home, Rimona, would shiver across the parents' visions. There were streets facing an ocean.
Marketplaces and piers where they played as children. And quickly, like a sneeze passing,
they were remembering white, and immersing themselves in the children's descriptions.

*

One of the reclining adults, an older woman, whose name was Germany, said to the children, *please, we need homes.*
So the children began to build triangular houses,
made from the supple branches of the freshly hardened trees
(hinges, sloping walls, doors, fireplaces, stoves, workshops, windows . . .).

*

As they built the homes, the children began to wonder if they could outpace the islands' natural rate of growth.
So they worked harder, assembling homes, while the island became lusher and lusher, hour by hour. Would their rates of growth ever meet?

VI
BROKEN SIMILE

Like Rimona, the parents thought. Echoed. Through a thick fog. Before the white ocean.
It was remarkably "like Rimona."
The flower you say. The flower we smell. The bird you say. The bird we hear. This is like Rimona.
Like Rimona. All the parents nodded and smiled in blind recognition, content with what they had always known.
The men & the women alike ventured to make analogy. This is like our coasts, our cliffs; this is like our trees, our flowers. This is like Rimona.
This is what we've always known.

VII
VIVIDNESS

The adults, whose sensitivities were deepening, felt the houses with their fingers, felt the trees with their fingers.
They were amazed to find that the materials they were touching matched the descriptions the children were giving.

*

They listened to the children working, joyfully and diligently. When the children had to pause to eat, when they couldn't do anything else but describe,
they looked around and described the trees and, as they did,
the bark became more intricate as the parents imagined it (and more tender when they felt it).

And sometimes when purple flowers and green leaves were given to the parents as gifts, they touched them and they imagined them as more
brilliant than the greens and purples of memory.

*

It was a kind of lull. A living dream.
The landscape was still rapidly greening.
And yellow fruit appeared, pearling from tree branches, which they feasted on eagerly.
A child called out, restlessly. She said, *We should name the island Vividness*. The other children whispered in agreement.
So they named the island *Vividness*.
And the name of the island was *Vividness*.

VIII
THE YELLOW FRUIT

After some time, the children began to feel a new sensation. The feeling that there was nothing else to say.
A feeling like falling. A fear forming like stone. An emptiness lining vision.
Yet whenever they ate the yellow fruit more descriptions returned to them. The fear of nothing vanished. So they ate the yellow fruit all the time.

*

Suddenly, a man named Granada said, *We must rebuild our numbers, we must procreate; we need more children to aid our children. Too few of us can see.*
So he directed the flow of reproduction on the island.
More and more children were born.

IX
GENERATION TWO

The travelers gave birth to more and more children. Pregnancy took weeks, not months. Sex was simple and effective.
Each child was born with two eyes, one in each socket.
They saw their parents in the ecstasy of renewal and rest. They tasted, smelled, and touched, ravenously. Sight was a sacrifice that now seemed unavoidable.
Rumors began to spread
        of parents turning back and walking into the sea, never to return
        of their brothers and sisters being eaten in the voyage over
The island was still stabilizing; the yellow fruit was still falling from trees. The fruit had no taste, but it seemed to satisfy them. The emptiness they felt when they stopped describing, however, persisted, and kept gnawing at them like a stone growing larger and larger in their throat.

X
SILVER MOUNTAIN

One day, in the clearing, a Silver Mountain rose out of the earth like a violent whale.
It stood still, and the people around it were confident — when they saw its silvery brilliance — that it would remain standing for a very long time.
It was beautiful. And its silver metal, they learned, could be melted and consumed to *heal the hunger for remembering home.*
Until then, the loop of description was the only way they knew how to distract themselves from *remembering.*

Who would collect the silver? Who would cook it?
The first generation only knew about seeing, describing, and building; they had never truly worked.
So the women gave birth to more children.

The island's population had grown. So the blind elders, in a flash of insight, decided to paint the bodies of half of the children *silver.*

And they decided to make the silver children work for the un-silvered people.
And so they enslaved their silver children.
And thus the silver children were enslaved.

The Silver Mountain seems to replenish itself, a young silver child said to a child who was not silver. And the child-who-wasn't-silver seemed to hear, but couldn't find the words to respond.
The silver one added, *It never goes down.*

When the children worked at the Silver Mountain, the other people could not see the difference between their silver bodies and the Silver Mountain itself; and none of it could be distinguished from what was retrieved.
From a distance it seemed like there was nothing, just a subtle texture, like mold on a root, or aphids on a leaf: Everything was silver.

XI
THE MINES

From a distance, on most days, the Silver Mountain was so bright that it was painful to look at.

The sunlight gleamed off its surface: searing reflective light.

The Rimonans were amazed to learn that the mountain's interior was also luminous; the "silver substance" seemed to ricochet sunlight into its inner depths. The mines — the tunnels that were built for the retrieval of silver metal — were corridors of endless, naked light.

They were so bright some of the silver children had to close their eyes as they entered and walked down corridors; they often would trace their fingers along the walls to make sure they were following the right tunnel down. Others covered their eyes with their hands as they walked.

(Some called the mountain *the mirror*; others called it *the mirror mountain*. Others called it *the miners' mirror*, or *the town's mirror*, or *the Rimonans' mirror*; some simply called it *a painful miracle*; in any case: depth into surface, surface into depth; the more depth revealed, the more light gleamed back at them, revealing more and more surface.)

When they emerged from the mines, with their backs to the mountain, they would open their eyes again. In their arms, they carried heaps of silver: gifts for the *un-silvered* people in the Triangular Village, which was rich with triangular sound: talking, discussion and description, and always hungering for home (and silver).

(The elders, still blind, were always rapt in the noise of description.)

From a distance, in their homes, the rest of the island, facing them expectantly, could not discern the silver children from the silver gifts they bore. Their skin against the mountain against the gift they held: silver.

They would cry: *O, look at all the silver. O, our souls have returned.*

But the silver children looked at the earth, and they felt that the earth saw them. Even though they could have washed the silver off themselves, they chose to keep it, since it made a distance between their skin and the earth — slightly further than their neighbors.

This gave them some comfort.

And this comfort was a wedge that formed two cultures.

In the triangular homes, they cooked the silver to cure their souls. They prepared it with the empty sustenance of the yellow fruit. They feasted. They were satisfied.

XII
THE SKY IS BLUE

One morning, the sky turned blue

XIII
THE LOVERS

Years pass.

Generations come and go.

One afternoon, on the way back home with a load of silver, a silvered man walked past an un-silvered man who was waiting for him with description. It was at this juncture in the production of silver that they would meet every day.

But instead of speech, they saw each other: two workers: a silvered man carrying silver, an un-silvered man carrying description. They didn't exchange anything; they slipped away from the path between Silver Mountain and Triangular Village, to the side of the island where there was an un-peopled shore (a shore without-home).

The noise of description was far away.

A relative silence. *A shore of the song.*

There was a beach with light beige sand. They couldn't avoid each other. Soon they became the whole image of each other.

There were women nearby, one was eating a yellow fruit by herself. She was looking out at the blue ocean. She seemed to be listening for the small particles of description as they wafted their way down from the center of the island to the empty beach. She looked up at the men as they walked down the slope of the beach.

They stood next to each other.

They waited until night fell and the earth felt settled. They looked down the rocks for a cave to hide in for the night.

While he hid from work, he nibbled at the piece of the Silver Mountain, and they were satisfied for days.

When they woke, they were near each other. The sirens that called the silver men and women into work were ringing. They shut their eyes, and kept sleeping.

Noon passed. Night passed. Morning passed.

They woke again.

Their hands were on each other.

XIV
A DIALOGUE

The silvered man said: *when I was in the mines*

I would
call orders to
other silver people
who would describe
what they saw
from
a lower mine

Now, my mind is white
mine of white mine of silver

       The un-silvered said: *why silver?*

            The silver was a
            way of gathering
            strength in reflection — to feel control
                     to cover something was to render it more deeply

Night fell again. *The sky was black.*

The silvered said:
the night was like a lower mine, to harvest,
cavities of doubt, cavities of light, to extract and build from.

His mind: a mine
lower layers to surface
of pleasure and control
surface into surface

They wanted to tell more. But they were tired.

They slept;
the two men were afraid of one another and touched again
and he leaned in to hear his rattling heart / my rattling heart.

Suddenly, it was the force of waves against fresh shores. The light wake of a child facing ocean.
Tracing toe in water.
Free, inquiring, nervous against great tenderness.

They sat; one hand on flaccid genitals, the other on genitals as firm as the first stone.
They held each other.

(Then it was the force of the brutal true lost laugh lowering into core) desire
The hand gripped arm. Hand on hand. The silver fell.
sigh; ejaculate; silver; fell

The silver fell.

[He had no name]

He had no name.
and he had no name
he and he had no name
had no name, he and he.
had no name, he.
Had no name, had no name.
he had no name. Name he. He
name he. Name name name. He had no. No he. He no. No
He had. had. he.
He had none. he no. He no. Nomós. Nome name.

[I'm Sorry]

I'm sorry

for the violence

in my voice

I know

you have

it too

The white water lapped at the shore.
It was the season when Silver Mountain was so bright it could burn your eyes if you looked directly.
It was still morning when they began to hear a song in another language from a distance.
New travelers were approaching the island.

XV
BREATHING LESSONS

In the morning light, against the wake, the new travelers reached the shore;
they arrived on motorized boats, dressed in all white.
And when they landed, they spoke to the lovers.

We hide here at night too. We have a lesson to give you.
We learned it from our god, our single parent, on the white ocean:
You do not need the yellow fruit for description or the scraps of Silver Mountain to abate emptiness.
That food is not food.
To purify yourself, you must learn how to be under water.

Under water, the pleasure of death will be felt more deeply,
and the fixations on pleasures of life will be loosened.

At the ocean floor
there will be nothing to retrieve.
Nothing to serve.
Nothing to describe.

Just the force of the trials of breath.

The lovers called this *The Breathing Trials*. With a partner back on a shore,
an anchor in the real, each swimmer attempts to swim to the ocean floor.
And with each trial, they sank down further and sang more deeply.

Until they felt the coral at the base of the island.

BREATHING TRIAL I

The silvered man, with silver paint flaking,
stood on a rock, took a breath
and dove into the white ocean.

As he sank deeper,
he sang in fearless exhalations:

I wrestled
the wire
angel

The angel
of memory

To open up
more time

It was an impossible time
It was impossible time

Break the voice
Break the voice
Break the mind

Enter into impossible silence
Give flesh to flatness

How to make
Time

To make the pressure
Positive

Rather than a squelching or
Overabundance

Community
An optical trick

*

How to make
the image
that is us?

Listen to
other languages

Their music
is not
your music

From them you learn
you have no music

To have no music
To have no language

Is to make song
Is to make the need for song

*

Wrestle
the wire angel

The angel
of memory

Until there are
no memories
left
no selves
left

To wrestle
oneself
from
oneself

BREATHING TRIAL II

how to hold breath
to go far enough

and come back
still breathing

to reach the root
in darkness

with memory of light
warmth, carried in you

skin cold
skin told

below the surface

the swimmers look around
there are forms
shapes, shadows,

forms of earth they had once thought would
resemble the white sky

they think now

that the coral looks like
an empty
Rimona
the Rimonans were the first sufferers
the first to leave
the neck
of
Europe
first to
begin to
replicate
disseminate
their europe
these are the swimmers swimming
down down down
they see the thread it is the
back of the eye
the root
the optic nerve

it has been watching us
every move
as we've built
every move
as we've decided
every move
described
this cascade of choices
we call our story
is vision to it
the lovers
turn from the coral
apparition
the apparition of earth
the skin cold
their breath nearly empty
they say to each other
in gesture
let's reach the bottom

above,
bodies float
some gasp for air
some have been emptied
vomit
those living
describe
a pure feeling
purification
purity
of having pressed themselves
into this
cold place

religion forms
we need to breathe less
to go deeper
to not eat these scraps of mountain

the lovers return
they do not have breath
but they are alive

they listen
they don't describe

they don't tell

BREATHING TRIAL III

the lovers
go down again
this time
hands held
to the bottom
to find
the root of the eye
the optic nerve

with two sets of hands,
they pull & pull & pull
to uproot the eye

as they touch it
it sends signals
messages
to the island above
the Rimonans
feel
a shock
it is the shock
that comes without-cause to them
(how to cause the feeling of *without-cause* in another?)
and it makes them feel
a world
flickering
with a deeper vividness
lifting its apparitional sheath

bring back the whale / whole
bring back the mountain
bring back the
eyes the island
bring back
the ocean
the voyage / voyage
bring back
the time before deciding
bring back
Rimona
bring back
us
can we
return
to
the noun
the proper noun
the proper noun of love?

XVI
THE WORLD IS DARK

The coral was white. It seemed to be looking at them.
The earth saw us.
They rushed up to the surface.
It felt like their skulls and lungs were collapsing as they emerged. They saw the blue sky.
They saw other swimmers. They were gasping for air.
The silver man said to his lover:

It told me to dig
with an optic blade
to take the eye
out of optic hole.

He shows him the blue eye.

The ocean was dark; the sky was dark.
There were copper stars glinting in the sky. The silver children and their families were glistening vividly.
The village, which had been gathering silver for generations, had barely whittled down the Silver Mountain at all
when the darkness fell.
The island started to shudder. The Rimonans fell into the ocean. Few could swim.
It had been so long since any of them had been at sea.
The lovers swam quickly. The island was collapsing; wake was forming. There was the noise of description; but it fell into the noise of night. No one seemed
to fear. Suddenly they were all under water, and they didn't need to breathe.
They felt the fin of something vast. Darkness.
They called it Whale, Vividness, Full-eye.
Sun eyes.
They bit its skin; they held onto it. It led them. It was force. The ocean was black.

BREATHING TRIAL IV

the ocean was black

or was it blue

or was it

green

or was it

gray

or was it

bright orange

or was it purple

or was it

yellow fruit red fruit

the throughout of a laugh

the ocean was the golden year

that never passed

XVII
THE PROPER NOUN OF LOVE

The silvered man began to sing

I began by describing the wrong tree. Its shadow is the tree falling.
I am the earth that has been shifted by the tree's falling shadow.
I began by removing the root of the word. Why had we ever moved?

Singing the song the birds stole
from the trees.

Singing the words the trees stole
from the birds.

Singing the trees the song stole
from the word.

The proper noun of love

Singing the word the trees had stolen
from the song

Singing the song the word had stolen
from the trees

The proper noun of love

Singing the song the trees had stolen
from the word

Singing the birds the word had stolen
from the song

Singing the word the trees had stolen
from the birds

The proper noun of love

LOSS
LESS
NESS

(Memoryless. Dreamless.)
—Theresa Hak Kyung Cha

Sans racines. Cent racines.
—Edmond Jabès

PROTI | ANTIGONI | HALKI | PRINQUIPO

from: Yvette Haviv <yvehav@gmail.com> date: Tue, Apr 12, 2016 at 1:49 PM to: Tom Haviv <tmhaviv@gmail.com>

Dear Tom,

I try as hard as I can
to prevent a spider
from installing his web
(although delicate)
on my mind, my memory.
89 in 4 months.
Here and there
flashbacks
of childhood —
what I was told,
school, Istanbul, the islands —
Proti, Antigoni, Halki, Prinquipo.
The sea
everywhere . . .
swimming, dancing
in the evenings.
Before that
much before
in a southern little town
by the Mediterranean.
The beach, delight
in plunging
into high waves,
coming out, waiting
for another wave . . .
The sea
always calm —
lying on it —
eyes closed seeing
colors, eyes
opened eyes
closed. You play
water carrying
you, embracing you.

Love, Yvette

A SIMPLE WORD

Voice recording of Yvette
(2015)

I have the impression
of losing something
of my vocabulary.

You know, one night
I was looking for a word.

I thought of a word, I don't
even remember which one . . .

I tried to find it
in French, I couldn't
in English, I couldn't
in Turkish, I couldn't

I couldn't sleep.

I said why try so hard?
It was 3 a.m. and I opened

the computer, put
it into Google
and I found it.

On the other hand
it may be good to find

it by thinking, by trying to remember,
but then maybe by opening the computer
it is better to choose the easy way,
since I wanted to sleep.

It was a simple word.
I can't remember it now.

AHMET | MELAHAT

from: Yvette Haviv <yvehaviv@gmail.com> date: Tue, Apr 12, 2016 at 1:49 PM to: Tom Haviv <tmhaviv@gmail.com>

Dear dear Tom,
I understand
you have decided
to energize
my memory,
keep it alive,
maybe adding
new neurons?
To counter-
balance
my fatigue?
I am waiting
for your
questions.

I was about 8.
The name
of the "boyfriend"
was Ahmet.
Same age.
From an eternity,
misty distance,
I see a round face,
kind of light
"peachy" cheeks
dark eyes . . .
I began
my schooling
in Mersin . . .
We used to
walk to school
come back together . . .
Once he took me to
his grandmother, living?
Not far . . .
A large courtyard —
one-story house?
Grandmother
sitting among
pillows on a low bench . . .
Ahmet knelt and
kissed her hand,
I was standing
by the door
(was shy in those times).
She made a sign to approach . . .

I came I knelt
kissed her hand —
imitating Ahmet . . .
She gave us some candies
At those times
"boyfriend or girlfriend"
had a different meaning
in French, in Turkish:
ami, amie, arkadaş
(not kız arkadaşim
or erkek arkadaşim).
While walking, Ahmet
and I talked nonstop.
Et voilà toute l'histoire
de l'amitié enfantine . . .

À 11 ou 12 ans
j'avais
(toujours à Mersin)
une camarade voisine,
Melahat, chez qui j'allais . . .
Elle était presque
obsedée
par le "modernisme"
— me posait
mille questions
sur les splendeurs
d'Istanbul lorsque
je revenais
des vacances
chez ma grandmère.
Nous étions comme
beaucoup
des admirateurs d'Atatürk
(décédé en 1938).
Melahat était brune
peut-être un peu plus agée
que moi.
Elle m'offrait du thé,
des bonbons, du "simit"
un genre de galette . . .

Tu vois Tom chéri
je n'arrête pas la "parlotte"!
Je suis passé au français
sans me rendre compte!
I love you, many
hugs and kisses.

MOISE

Voice recording of Yvette
(2015)

In those confused
times, the '30s,
the only person
in the family
preoccupied
by actualities
was my grandfather
Moise Benusiglio.
1936. When Mussolini
occupied Ethiopia,
he was so upset;
he predicted
the worst for Europe.
These events
and the
fate of the
Jews marked
my life as a
young girl
in Istanbul.
And also
the unrest
in Istanbul;
some families
fled to the south
for fear of German
invasion.

DAVID | GILDA

Voice recording of Yvette
(2015)

When the Nazis
took Greece (1941),
my two uncles,
the elder brothers
of my mother,
Joseph & David,
were there and
they went in hiding
in the villages.
They were hidden by
the Athenian villagers.
But David's wife
Gilda was able
to leave because
she was a Turkish citizen,
and the Turkish consulates
everywhere
allowed the Jews
who had Turkish
nationality
to go to Turkey.
So my aunt
and my cousin,
I don't know
if you met him,
they came to Istanbul.
One of my uncles, David,
who had been
born in Saloniki
escaped —
illegally arrived in Palestine.
What the British did
to Palestine
I will never
forgive them.

BLACKED OUT WINDOWS

Voice recording of Yvette
(2015)

The Germans
had already taken
Greece
and Yugoslavia.
Bulgaria.
And they were
on the border of
Turkey.
But the Turkish
government
declared
neutrality.
The Romanians
were conquered.
Because
Hitler
didn't respect
any
accord
so we were
expecting
this war.

why did they black out the windows?

We blacked
out windows.
It was a way of
defending
from air attacks.
And as the Nazis
were already
at the border,
we were given
orders
to be careful
and also
to make a reserve
of bread,
since there was no
bread anymore.

They began
rationing the food
in case there
is an invasion.

You know
in my family also
we had two aunts
the wives of my uncles
they were thinking already
to leave Istanbul
and go south
because of the danger.

But then
the Germans stopped
and went to the Russian front
and there was
no invasion.

There was tension,
tension
something
in the atmosphere.

Istanbul was a
a city full of spies.
It was a very important
city strategically
between the Black Sea
the Aegean
and the Mediterranean Sea . . .

MAH | SUSANNE

Voice recording of Yvette
(2017)

During the war
in Turkey,
we had a neighbor,
she was Turkish.
She was the wife
of a very famous
Turkish officer.
They lived downstairs.
We had a maid
Susanne.
She was grilling
by the window
and she had some laundry down there
and she came downstairs to complain.
Our maid
Susanne
who was Jewish,
she had chutzpah,
opened her mouth against the mistress.
And this woman
told the police
or her husband.
All of a sudden
the police came
to our house
and wanted to talk
to me and to my mother.
They took us to the
police station
in the middle of the night.
I was 14.
So it seems
like this woman
did something
and her powerful
husband
told the police to do this.
It was unjust
and no reason at all,
after all a
14-year-old girl.
The next day
they let us go home.
They said tomorrow

to go to
the MAH
Milli Emniyet Hizmeti
(like the FBI or Shabak)
and we went.

There were three
people sitting
there
and they said
why do you do this?
You are Turkish.
And my mother
did not know
Turkish well,
she opened her mouth.

There was
an earthquake
terrible
in the east of Turkey.
We were
in the south
in Mersin.
My mother worked
hard to send
clothes
to the persons
who were injured.
And they gave
her a medal.

She also gave
her ring
as a contribution.
It was
her wedding ring
and it was
white gold
beautiful.

So when they called her,
she said to the three men
*Which one of your wives
gave their wedding ring?*

They didn't say anything.
She really
had chutzpah.

MÈRE EMMANUELLE | SHEMA

Voice recording of Yvette
(2015)

In 1943,
our schoolteacher
in Notre Dame de Sion
in Istanbul
was Mère Emmanuelle,
a nun and
an extraordinary woman
of Belgian origin.
She taught all the students —
Catholic, Muslim, Jewish —
leçons générales . . .
But she gave us
Jewish students
les leçons morales
(ethics)
each week.
We took it by
choice; it was
not an obligation
to take the course.

One day
she said to us,
Your
brothers and sisters
in Europe
are going
through a
very bad
situation.
You must pray
for them
every night.
(She said, *It is*
important
to pray,
even if
you are
not used
to praying.)
So she wrote
on the blackboard

in Latin characters
the words
of the prayer
she wanted us to make.
And it went:

Shema Yisrael Adonai Eloheinu . . .

It turns out
she had spoken
to a rabbi
to choose a prayer . . .

Yet as soon as
she wrote it,
it was erased.

Why? At the time
it was forbidden
by the new government
to have any lessons
of religion.
The director
of the school
from the ministry
of education
was watching —
always watching.

But we prayed it
together then.

It was my first prayer.

I prayed it
each evening
until the end
of the war . . .

LIZANKA | YVETTE | BELLA

Voice recording of Yvette
(2017)

I was about 15.
I was in the 10th grade.
Two friends
came from another
school.
One of them was active
in the
Zionist movement.
So she
approached us,
me and the other girl.
We were about
ten Jewish girls
in our class.
Except me,
the others didn't
really care
so much
about
Jewishness
or the pogroms.
Nothing.
They were not
interested.
But when she
came . . .
Lizanka
she was
Jewish from
Bulgarian
origin.
And Bella,
her father came from Russia,
and her mother from Istanbul.
They became my friends.

And Lizanka took
the two of us
and began to tell
us about
the organization,
about the idea

of having a place
for the Jews
according to
the Balfour Declaration.

And so
this movement
prepared people,
young people,
Jewish, who wanted
to help the creation
of the place
for the Jews
and to go
to Palestine.

IZZY | ISLANDS | ALICE

Voice recording of Yvette
(2017)

I entered
the Zionist
movement.
They organized
trips by boat.
You know?
Those boats
that go
to the
Bosphorus
to the
islands.

It was a boat
traveling between
the Bosphorus
and going to
different places. We
had an excursion,
a picnic,
organized
in one island
and we got down.

I was
for the first time
on such a boat
with the others
and Izzy
was there.

He was
on one side
of the boat,
I was
on the other.

I didn't know anybody
except for my two friends.

From afar
we smiled
at each other.
And after
we began
to be active
together.

After that,
I was very sick
for two months. I had
a very serious kind of tuberculosis.
At this time, there was
no penicillin, not in Istanbul.
I was in bed for two months.
My parents took a house
in one of the Islands
and I was there. Izzy and friends
would come and visit me. Izzy
would come very often. We used
to have talks; that was the beginning
of our friendship.

When it turned out to be girlfriend . . .
you know, when he escaped,
and they caught him,
and he came back, so before
he left, then we told
each other . . . he told me
that he loves me,
and I love him,
and I promised
when he comes to
Palestine, I will
follow him.
Of course, I didn't say this to my mother.
My mother didn't want
me to go out with Izzy
because she knew
he would continue
with his adventure. She didn't
want me to be with him, so I
would not leave. She was
against all my activities. My father
understood a little more.
I can understand my mother
because I had lung problems,
because the climate was not good.

But we were motivated
to go and help
build the State
and to the great, great
sadness of my parents
who really didn't want me to go
and for the first time
I really made them very
. . . especially my mother.
She was very far from
the Zionist idea.

from: Yvette Haviv <yvehav@gmail.com> date: Sun, Mar 15, 2015 at 12:52 PM to: Tom Haviv <tmhaviv@gmail.com>

SHAAR ALIYAH | MOUNT CARMEL

Izzy.
We lived
together
65 years.
עם הדבש והעוקץ
(with the honey
and the bee sting).
And met
three years
before, 1946.

Why
did it take me
some time
to write about him?
I miss him.
I feel him
strongly engraved
in my memory.
If I write
about the "hardships"
in his life
since the age of 27,
he would refute
and say just
"some problems."

Our arrival
in the
newly founded state
by boat
(you have our photograph)
the Anne Marie.
With many
other immigrants,
the port of Haifa,
the emotion
we both felt was very
special,
I feel it now while writing.
Izzy was 22.
I was 21.
One week
after our simple
wedding

at my parents'
home — my home
also.
Rejoicing and
sadness too.
Leaving
our parents, our loving
families, friends.
(In the boat, I cried
a lot, conscious
of the pain
I was causing
my wonderful
father and mother,
my little sister.)

They took
all of us
to a place
called
Shaar Aliyah.
Tents, tents, and tents . . .
While in the boat
four girls older than us
became friendly with me.
When we all arrived
to the Immigrant's Gate,
they suggested we find
a big tent for all of us.

When Izzy heard,
he took my hand
and fast we went
searching for a smaller tent.
The smallest had three beds.
He found one.
Two beds and the third
completely broken.
After all it was still
our honeymoon!

The situation
in the camp
was not easy.
The residents were
from other countries too.
Iraq, Iran, Romania,

each one different
from the other.
Ladies with *tarbush*
on their heads, wearing
the oriental *shalwar* . . .
No common language,
they spoke
Arabic, Kurdish, Polish . . .

Thousands . . .
the distribution
of food
was a *balagan.*

Izzy and I
managed with dry fruits
we brought with us,
some cookies . . .
and of course
Turkish coffee.
The food was scarce in Israel.
The population
was 600,000 —
more than
a million immigrants arrived.
So the new government
decided for food rationing.

Let's have
some coffee,
says Izzy. How?
Izzy had brought
a *fincan & cezve.*
There was water
out of the tents.
No cooker, no fire . . .
He takes two or three hazelnuts
puts them in an aluminum plate
he had matches
being a smoker,
lit the nuts,
put water coffee sugar
in the *cezve*, and we enjoyed the best
Turkish coffee ever,
with some cookies.
Les petits plaisirs de la vie.

All of a sudden
we see
David and Gilda
(aunt and uncle)
searching for us
among the tents.
It appears that
my uncle went
to the Jewish Agency,
the authority
for new immigrants,
learned that the Anne Marie
arrived on time,
and according
to the travelers' list
"their children" were transferred
to Shaar Aliyah.
It was not easy
for them to come
by bus from
Tel Aviv to Haifa
from there
the bus up
to the camp on
Mount Carmel.
They immediately
took us out of the camp
(with our three suitcases)
to the bus for Tel Aviv.
Was it a dream?
The old bus advancing
slowly along the coast
of the Mediterranean,
the breathtaking sunset
colors
red, orange, mauve,
splashed
over the blue
tranquil ocean,
a surge of joy,
the rhythmic
pounding of
my heart (was there
in the world
some place
more beautiful?).

Hello Tom
Thank you
for your kind
encouraging
email.

I feel I have
to touch
a painfully hidden
in my heart
memory-event:
Izzy's eyes.
Beginning
in 1953, the
partial loss
of vision field
in his one eye.
Tests couldn't
determine the
cause. There was no
CT or MRI then.
In 1959, same thing
in the second eye.
We were in Ethiopia
at the end of our mission.
We heard of a
prominent eye
specialist in Geneva.
Our good friends
posted there
contacted him, and
Izzy left for Geneva.

How long was he
in that clinic?
In retrospect
it seemed like ages!
He underwent tests.
The result: again
same diagnosis:
an infection
attacks
the optic nerve
and paralyzes it.
Why? How?

from: Yvette Haviv <yvehav@gmail.com> date: Mon, Jan 26, 2015 at 2:44 PM to: Tom Haviv <tmhaviv@gmail.com>

Maybe the second time,
a continuation
of the first attack?

A totally healthy
young man . . .

While he was in Geneva,
a well-known
neurosurgeon,
Prof. Beler
arrived to Addis Ababa,
invited by the emperor
to examine a member
of his family.
He was
at the embassy
I told him about Izzy's case.
He remembered it
as he had been in 1953
among the doctors
who examined Izzy.
He told me to contact
him as soon as
we arrive to Israel.
We did in 1959. His proposal:
a craniotomy (head surgery)
to see what was
the damage
(still no CT no MRI)
and maybe find a way
to prevent further deterioration . . .

But he explained clearly
that it should be Izzy's
decision as the surgery is dangerous . . .
we had no family in Israel.
Good friends, neighbors
from the ministry — some whispered
to me: Don't let him do it!
They helped take care of
Shlomo, three and a half,
Daniel, six
or seven months,
while I
was at the hospital
alone waiting waiting

until the end of the surgery.
When Beler appeared,
he told me: *I think*
I stopped the process,
I cleaned all around
the infected area . . .
He looked
very optimistic!
You imagine,
Tom, what I felt!
I sent him a big bunch
of flowers
as he did not charge
us even
one penny.

NO NAME

A dream I remember now:
I stand on the shore of a sea, ocean —
water covering
my feet . . . I want to advance, walk
and throw myself in, to swim and swim and
swim as far as possible — the way I used to
lose my body in the
water,
I am the sea, the Black Sea, the Bosphorus,
the Mediterranean, I
dive under it watching the
choreography of the fish
around me, then lying on my back to welcome
the sun rays,
close my eyes to see scintillating day stars,
dreaming,
diving again . . .
I stand still
on the shore yearning
to enter the sea . . .
My feet are stuck
I cannot
move them — a rock . . .
I remain with my almost
crying yearning . . .
Anxieté, angoisse!

from: Yvette Haviv <yvehav@gmail.com> date: Tue, Feb 21, 2017 at 9:05 PM to: Tom Haviv <tmhaviv@gmail.com>

PARIS | BURGAZ | BUCHAREST

1970
FRANCE

Izzy appointed
Economic Counselor
Israeli Embassy in Paris.

I didn't work.
Visiting Paris, all its
streets, boulevards,
Rive Gauche, Quartier Latin,
musées (Montparnasse,
well-known cafés where poets,
writers, painters were their
"habitués" like La Closerie,
Les Lilas, Café de Flore,
Les Deux Magots . . .
Café de la Paix near the Opéra).
Everything seemed
so familiar to me:
names of little plazas,
the people. Some as if
coming out
of the books
I had read.
Well I loved it.
Back home
at the hour
Shlomo and Daniel
returned
from school. It was
an Israeli school for
the children of the embassy.

1973. Back to Jerusalem
1974. Izzy, Ministry of Finance
          Yvette, Office of the President

1974
JERUSALEM

Yom Kippur War.
Traumatic.
Friends, neighbors lost
their sons.

(Amos)
I still remember
every detail of this
day — a lovely
sunny day.
On Kippur day:
no cars,
buses
or any other vehicle
seen in the
whole country —
except an ambulance
here and there
for emergency.
You can see
children, youngsters
riding their bicycles
or a group of people
next to a synagogue, or
people walking around
without apprehending
a car *klaxon*.
So at 11:00
I decided
to walk to a
friend's house.
Shlomo and Daniel
were with friends,
Izzy still in Paris. At 14:00
a car
goes by calling us
to open the radio. We did.
And listened. War. Prepare
the shelters,
put dark shades
on the windows.
Golda Meir
on TV announcing
the news:
We were attacked
by the Egyptians,
in the south,
the Syrians
in the north
and the Jordanians
from the east.
A traumatic surprise!

Israel after the victory
of the Six-Day War
had become too
self-confident, arrogant,
(Dayan)
and security was
neglected, and all the rest.
Kissinger interfered
initiated ceasefire talks,
then peace negotiations etc.

1974. Yitzhak Rabin, Prime Minister

Izzy loses
one eye totally,
remains
with 10% of vision
field in the second.
He teaches himself
to function,
walking, reading,
writing, playing bridge.
Doctors couldn't
understand how.
In their opinion
Izzy was blind,
or almost.
1977 retires
from the government.
He opens a crêperie
together with a friend.
They named it
Poire et Pomme.
A small restaurant,
an immediate success.
Then they opened
a larger one in a very
picturesque place
of Jerusalem.
Izzy was
the mind
behind this enterprise.
He was the
one who chose the
personnel — most of them
young friends
of Shlomo or Daniel.

BURGAZ | ISTANBUL

The year
of the opening,
my father,
very ill, came to
Jerusalem Hadassah
Hospital. Cancer.
He and my mother
decided to go back
to Istanbul. There
was no hope
of cure.
There his wonderful
Turkish physician
took care of him,
at home, coming regularly,
encouraging him,
keeping him
in a good mood.

Lily and I
decided
to come and
visit him
taking turns;
I took leave from work,
arrived in Istanbul.

He had passed away
the night before.
I still cannot
describe
the pain, the deep
sorrow I felt.

It had been very hard
for my mother.
They loved each
other so much!
Their marriage was one
of the most successful
I have witnessed.
My sister and I
came to visit
our parents
in Burgaz

(the island).
1976, my
dad's last summer.
I used to
accompany him
to the débarcadère
to the boat
for the city
where he still worked.
It is on one
of those mornings
that he said to me,
"Do you know
that you have
an extraordinary mother?"
He also was extraordinary.
He loved to study. At home
I never saw him without
a book in his hand.
He was an autodidact.
Son of a rabbi
he spent his youth
in Paris. Then came
back to Turkey
and worked at the
Banque de Salonique,
married my mother
Alice Benusiglio.
His French was
perfect, he learned English,
he spoke Ladino
as all the Spanish Jews,
he learned some German.
He could read Hebrew
and understand it,
and of course
Turkish. He was not
religious;
even at a young age,
atheist or free thinker.
At the age
of 40 came back to
tradition. He became
more interested
in Jewish history
and liked my
being Zionist.

All my mother's
family loved him.
His parents had died.
His brothers and sisters were far —
in Paris, in the U.S.
And so the Benusiglios adopted
him and he enjoyed
being with them.
My grandparents'
house in Istanbul
was called by
the neighbors
"La Casa de la Alegría"
as I was told later by
a neighbor. During WWI
they left Salonica to Naples.
They were happy there:
a lot of music, operas . . .
They learned to play the
guitar, the mandolin, they
sang and loved being there.
For financial reasons
they left and came to
Istanbul where lived
my grandma's brother
Emmanuel
(one of the
Young Turks
who revolted
against the sultan
of the Ottoman Empire)
who was a member of the
first Turkish parliament.
I have some wonderful
images
of those times
at my grandmother's.
Did I say
already that my parents
in the south of Turkey
sent me from time to
time to Istanbul?

I was accompanied
by a neighbor
or a friend of my
parents. The journey

by train — those old ones
when they used coal.
The train stopped
at a lot of stations.
People selling hot boiled fresh
corns, sugar-coated red
apples. Some selling
lovely, many-colored
peasants' scarves.
Others selling
fresh fruit juices.
The station full
of people, some
greeting the arrivals, some
who were there just for fun.
Right now here
I hear a train passing.
It makes me sad,
even tense, remembering
friends in Israel
who were in camps . . .
And the transport train . . .

Anyhow on the train
to Istanbul — I think it
was before the war.
Istanbul.
It used to be very
cosmopolitan.
Later I learned that
at that time
the city was full of spies.
Maybe I worked
with one of them. I'll
never know.

1960
ROMANIA

Izzy second secretary,
promoted later
to first secretary. Those
are diplomatic grades.
Romania was part of
the communist block
(Russia and
satellites — Poland,

Czechoslovakia,
Hungary,
Bulgaria, Romania)
for the western
block
including Israel,
serving in those
countries considered
"hardship
posts." We couldn't
speak freely.
Our apartments
were bugged,
in cars or walking —
each diplomat
had a follower
from the security.
The servants
or housekeepers
were provided
by the Romanian
foreign office.
We were aware
that their duty was
to report
everything related
to the family they worked for.
Our phone
talks were recorded.
So we had
to be careful
and evaded
long conversation.

We couldn't just talk,
in the street,
synagogue, park
to persons
we encountered
for fear of
endangering them,
being
accused of
western propaganda.
You could be declared
persona non grata,
then your

government had
to call you back
home.

But they
continued to keep
the traditional
"Diplomat's Club," which
existed much
before the current
regime,
a beautiful place
by Lake Băneasa.
This is where
we went all of us,
all the corps diplomatique,
(including their children);
you could
play tennis
volleyball, golf.
And talk freely.

A tense,
interesting
and also pleasant
period.
I can also
tell you the
difficulties and
hardships of the people:
scarcity of food,
a totalitarian regime,
less harsh than Russia
it was said . . .
Culture
was cheap —
concerts, theaters — but
controlled.

from: Yvette Haviv <yvehav@gmail.com> date: Sun, Feb 1, 2015 at 7:42 PM to: Tom Haviv <tmhaviv@gmail.com>

SHLOMO | OHIO

How are you?
Here white
is all around me.
On the west
side of my studio.
I watch
the pine tree leaves
wearing white gloves.
On them little black
button-eyes of a hidden tree.
Nature's inverse tricks:
one eye at the bottom,
another farther, a mouth
(smiling?) on top,
hanging white cold, oh so cold
fingers, hurt, longing for
defrost . . . like me.

What am I saying?
I am warm in my room,
opening the door
from time to time
and letting the fresh air
vivify my brain.
It seems that I've become
used to a solitary life,
even like it. But I love when every
week, Saturday or Sunday,
Shlomo brings
me to their house for lunch.

At home,
I try from time to time
to activate
my vocal cords.
As I don't speak
much, I wouldn't like them
to be more
rusted than usual at my age.
Do you know what I do?
I try to sing: high?
no let's try lower,
no — this sounds
false! Until I reach
approximately

the nice pleasant
voice Yvette Karillo
used to have.

Almost every day
Lily and I talk,
about our past,
common and different,
the wonderful family
we had, each one of us
mirroring different
views, aspects,
also she is five years
younger than me.
Both of us nostalgic
for our "magic"!
Istanbul . . .
Tomorrow: I
promise: Romania!

Love, grandma
Hoping you'll manage
in this "labyrinth."

LADDER ALLEGIANCE

I am the outskirts of a nonexistent town.
—Fernando Pessoa

Ainsi, toujours poussés vers des nouveaux rivages,
Dans la nuit éternelle emportés sans retour,
Ne pourrons-nous jamais sur l'océan des âges
Jeter l'ancre un seul jour?
—Alphonse de Lamartine | Yvette voice recording

LADDER

I

How does
a story break?

Not by
taking it
apart
(or dismantling it)

but by

telling and
retelling

and retelling.

The story
is a
bow
It is a string
It is a net
holding the weight
of fruit fallen
from old trees —
and it cannot hold.
I wake in a blanket
of sound & light
in a remote town where
the story of who owns what
the story of who took what
is told and retold
until the story breaks
on earshot
and the mind closes.

II

You are
standing
in a field
the soil
wet with
heavy rain
that has
just passed

*

You are
on a train
to work
the book
creased
but not yet
opened

*

You are
flying
home
head on
window

*

You are
having
dinner
with an
old friend

*

You are
forming
the words
to tell
the same
story
and it
breaks

*

In the field
the story
returns to you
a star: broken–shining–incoherent–singing
in a language
you can't identify
if it is
even in a language
known anywhere?

*

You are
talking
to a new
lover
and it breaks

*

It falls
falls
like a
ladder
kicked down
from a window

(*whereof one cannot speak thereof one must be silent*)

Do you
remember
where we
were both
left
standing?

*

You resist
the soldier
twists
your arms
your words
you yell
a word?

he yells
a word?
nothing builds
the story breaks

*

Your mother
tells you
a story

Before you
can make
out its
meaning
the story
breaks

III

At what point

    in its

      telling

does a story —

          break?
               by teeth, by tongue, by gum, by mouth?

the accumulated facts

          break

the whispered assurances

          break

the down-bending apology

          breaks

the incisive argument

          breaks

in 1945 the Americans liberate

          breaks

in 1948 we landed

          breaks

the story began in

      Istanbul

          breaks

the story began in

      Thessaloniki

          breaks

Auschwitz

        breaks

Córdoba

        breaks

Gaza

        breaks

Jerusalem

        breaks

IV

When it breaks

    silence
    fear / embarrassment
    jealousy / anguish

the lie bends not

the lie fractures, is no longer pliant

        breaks

we are here because

        breaks

they behave this way because

        breaks

they set fires

        breaks

our destiny is to

        breaks

we deserve this place

        breaks

this is how one survives

        breaks

this is how we learned to survive

        breaks

this is why they hate us

        breaks

this is just their culture

        breaks

when the story you were told

becomes brittle

        & breaks / barak / breaks / bracha

        breaks

V

The field
thickens
into a forest
the soldier is

leading you
out of the poem

He points ahead
over there
you will find nothing
no answers
to your questions
no richness lived in
no community

I suggest you go there

since it's where I'm from too

home.

VI

How long have you been telling this story?

The soldier presses.

Since childhood,

I say

They even told it
before
I was born

Why this story?

I am not the only one

the guilt
breaks

is it
faith
or is it
mute
fate?

Where are you from? M'efo atah?

The soldier asks.

[We walk further together | We feel each other's heat]

115

VII

You are speaking
to your lover
and the
words snap
at hinges
careless — you had
spoken again — that same
story — nothing altered
and under no weight
each word breaks

(if it is no longer
told, does it not break?
will it decompose?)

the life

                              breaks

the trust

                              breaks

the alibi

                              breaks

the carcass

                              breaks

                          (flies collect on grasshopper's carapace,
                                    grinding into grass
                   — the ant carries a smaller ant, raw material now, down.)

(the nation

                              breaks)

the good fight

                              breaks

the hysteria

                              breaks

the question

          breaks

the answer

          breaks

the friendship

          breaks

the lust

          breaks

the lesson

          breaks

the curriculum

          breaks

the poem

          breaks

the school

          breaks

the calculation

          breaks

the cunning

          breaks

the numbness

          breaks

the numbers

          break

the analysis

                              breaks

the noose

                              breaks

the power

                              breaks

the siege

                              breaks

the hand

                              breaks

the quiet

                              breaks

the threat

                              breaks

the treaty

                              breaks

the ceasefire

                              breaks

the call to prayer

                              breaks

the sabbath

                              breaks

the intention

                              breaks

the lineage

                            breaks

the history

                            breaks

the commitment

                            breaks

the covenant

                            breaks

the fear

                            breaks

the shame

                            breaks

the sorrow

                            breaks

the pity

                            breaks

the grief

                            breaks

the ladder

                            breaks

VIII

Do they break in constellation?

(or something more violent:
nettles in a crown or
sky-weapon)

do they break, falling into
earth — crystals of
kindness — as they
are no longer being told
& told & told & told & told
(not untold)

we let grieving overtake us

we let out grief like rain

we let out grief like rain

into the ruin
that nourishes
the earth — and

lets new life come out gently

                              (slowly, slowly)

finally

the
land
              sings as
              we let broken
              things be reclaimed by it.

ALLEGIANCE

HABIB | GERRERA | ACEMAN

1946. As soon as my grandfather graduates from *lycée*,
he and two close friends leave Istanbul in secret
and travel south to the new border of Turkey and Syria.

They want to make their way to Palestine.

In Palestine, a war is escalating.

Across the former Ottoman Empire, borders are flickering into being.

1923. The Turkish Nationalist Movement reclaims Anatolia led by Mustafa Kemal Atatürk;
       the Turkish republic forms.

1946. The French mandatory rule lifts;
       the Syrian and Lebanese republics form.

1946. Three boys receive draft notices from the Turkish military.

They decide to leave their state forever   evade their draft   and join a new army.

Panels of
white, blue, and red.
A cypress tree. A white disc.

The rise of the modern Turkish state
sets a new paradigm for Sephardi Jews
who had been living in the region for centuries,
the promise of a new ethno-national identity:

Turkishness.

This presents itself first in language.

Atatürk believed in Sun Language Theory,
which claimed that all human language derives from an originary Turkic language
spoken in ancient Sumer. This theory was as tenuous then as it is now,
but the result was the reconfiguration of the new secular state
around *Turkishness above all.*

For the first time in history, all schools in Anatolia were required to teach Turkish.
During the Ottoman Empire, under the *millet* system
(millet deriving from millah, *nation,* in Qur'anic Arabic),
minority groups had cultural and linguistic autonomy.

My family had been in the Ottoman Empire for 400 years.
They spoke, at different points, Greek, Arabic, French, Italian,
as well as Ladino, or Judeo-Spanish, the dialect of the Sephardim.
None of these languages were acceptable in the new state.

My grandmother, Yvette, was one of the first people to speak Turkish fluently in her family;
my grandfather, Israel, had been the second in his family; his father had served as an Ottoman officer in WWI.
For many reasons, this generation would find itself the last — or next to last — to speak Turkish.

A red and white flag.
Six arrows fanning outward,
as if generated by an invisible sun.

The *lycée* the boys went to was a significant part of the story as well.

It belonged to the *Alliance Israélite Universelle* system,
a schooling system created in 1860
to spread secular French education
and culture to Jewish communities
throughout the Ottoman Empire and the Middle East.

Its mission was to civilize,
to create for non-Ashkenazi Jews
a special relationship with
European "modern" civilization
vis-à-vis French language and culture.

Alliance schools spanned
all the way from Morocco to Iran and Afghanistan,
administering European influence,
bringing the so-called Oriental Jews into the Enlightenment
as Jews and making them useful and loyal colonial subjects.

A red and white flag.
A crescent and a star
at the center.

These three boys, whose last names were Habib, Gerrera, and Aceman, belonged to another emergent nationalist movement.

In Turkish and French they sang its name: *The Underground Zionist Youth Movement.*

1923. The new Turkish state criminalizes all Zionist activity.

Prior to the fall of the Ottoman Empire, the struggle to convince Sephardi communities to become Zionist had not been easy.
It had been a public fight between European Zionists, French colonial Jews, Greek & Turkish nationalists — many of whom were Jews — the Ottoman establishment, and the Sephardi rabbinate. After Atatürk came to power, this complexity — *a wing* — would narrow to a pointed collision of two ideologies, two theories of peoplehood: Turkish nationalism and Zionism.

In Turkey, many were in the throes of *becoming Turkish* for the first time.

In the eyes of the state — *arrows* — Zionism was a counter-nationalism that threatened the cohesion of the whole. We now know:
these nationalisms were, in fact, mirrors of each other — *narrowing* — echoes of a European-style nationalism that had never previously entered the Middle East.

Seven yellow stars.
Two bands of blue.
White background.

My grandparents conducted their activism in secret from their families; being part of this work, or even implicated, could threaten lives and livelihoods.

According to my grandmother, when they knocked on doors, most Jews turned them away — *a wing*. The notion of a new identity was not compelling to everyone. For hundreds of years, many had been very comfortable with being *Ottoman* — as that empire was often seen by Sephardim as the beloved redeemer of those fallen from the Iberian Peninsula. Now they had to decide between *becoming Turkish* or *becoming Zionist*.

They spent hundreds of years becoming — why leave?

From a cousin, the summer of 2018 in Rosh HaAyin, I learn that there were Sephardi Rabbis — *arrows* — in the '50s and '60s still imploring Jews in Ladino to move to Israel. Many of these Jews stayed even as tensions rose; all but one of my great-grandparents, my grandmother's mother, Alice, would spend their final years in Istanbul.

Today, the Jewish community in Turkey — *narrowing* — is the second largest remaining Jewish community in the Middle East after Israel.

A red triangle
against three color panels.
Green. White. Black.

CHEMIN DE RÊVE

They made
their way
to the border
with a dream.
They wanted
to pass
through Syria,
Lebanon, into
Palestine,
to join
an armed struggle
that would create
a Jewish
nation state.

What had the boys imagined of the slopes of Syria and Lebanon?

On the way to the border, they stopped in the city of Antalya
where they met a border guard who had agreed to help smuggle them over for a fee.
Then, as my father tells me, they chose to stay for a night, or maybe for a few days, we don't know.
They needed a rest.
        Did they wonder if they could step outside of history?
If only for a day / *un seul jour?*

Did they know they would never make it over?

Were they Turks? Were they Jews? Were they Ottomans?
Were they Israelis? Were they Hebrews?
Human forms in a landscape, moving through darkness, pausing in a clearing of light.
They were all those who had been born into war, whose choice was one nation or another; nation for nation; nation over nation;
windows narrowing / windows closing
they too deserved their adolescence.

Did they know there was no pathway back?

May 1948. Two weeks after the Yishuv announced the "independence" of a Jewish state, Martin Buber wrote in an article that Zionism had died. He wrote that he feared a Jewish victory would be the downfall of Zionism. Buber, a recent arrival in Palestine from the collapsed German Jewish world, is most commonly remembered as a scholar and philosopher. Lesser known is the fact that he was also an active proponent of a radical version of Zionism that, in a sense, lost the battle

for the Jewish imagination. He helped establish a binationalist Zionist group called the Brit Shalom, which advocated for a shared nation of two peoples based on socialism and an integrated economy and government. He argued against "nationalist assimilation," by which he meant mere European nationalism — the nationalism that had exterminated European Jewry.

The article from May 1948 was titled "Zionism and 'Zionism'":

"Fifty years ago, when I joined the Zionist movement for the rebirth of Israel, my heart was whole. Today it is torn. The war being waged for a political structure risks becoming a war of national survival at any moment. Thus against my will I participate in it with my own being, and my heart trembles like that of any other Israeli. I cannot, however, even be joyful in anticipating victory, for I fear lest the significance of Jewish victory be the downfall of Zionism . . .

This sort of 'Zionism' blasphemes the name of Zion; it is nothing more than one of the crude forms of nationalism, which acknowledge no taste above the apparent (!) interest of the nation. Let us say that it is revealed as a form of national assimilation, more dangerous than individual assimilation; for the latter only harms the individuals and families who assimilate, whereas national assimilation erodes the nucleus of Israel's independence."

What borders formed
around their imagination?
What borders form around ours?

THE OBSTACLE OF MYTH

A window
in the wall

opens
narrows
closes

an eye

a myth
opens
narrows
closes

Which windows remain?
Which walls?
Will we name them?

I used to say

    the Israeli state betrayed my family.

                  Their vision, their dream.

I wonder
    is the truth
        simply
           that stories change,

               and no single story will ever bring us to the promised land?

In the morning, they went toward the border.
As soon as they did,
they were arrested,
ratted out | הלשינו עליהם
and were immediately
sent to a military prison back in Antalya.

The borders of imagination have closed since.

In prison, my grandfather Israel Habib and his two friends Bulent Aceman and Yaacov Gerrera ate feta, olives, tomatoes, and bread, and, as my grandfather would tell me, were happy. The way this was conveyed to me has the trace of his dark humor and pride; his dignity that would follow him over thresholds of trouble; his hard-earned lack of faith.

They were charged with committing two crimes: evading the Turkish military draft and participating in the illegal Zionist movement.

When they faced the judge, according to family folklore, my grandfather was asked to speak on behalf of the three boys. He is said to have made a rousing case for their mission, their dream: *you have established your state, now we deserve ours. Unlike our parents, who were Ottomans first, Jews second, we are now Jews above all else*: we deserve to return to our own history.

Did they know there was no pathway back?

CHEMIN DE LA MER

When they were released, they returned to Istanbul where Israel was arrested again and further interrogated and beaten. They considered him the leader of the trio; they wanted to know who else would be conspiring to leave the state.

*

Because he had clout the others did not, Aceman's father pulled some strings with the security forces, and Israel was freed. Part of their agreement upon release was that they would each complete the year of military service that they had attempted to evade. In the end, Israel spent six months at the officers' academy and six months in the Turkish Air Force as a liaison with the US Air Force. My father tells me that my grandfather wrote a pamphlet in Turkish for how to play bridge for the other Turkish-speaking officers that was disseminated widely. Bridge was an abiding passion through his old age.

*

1948. The state emerges out of the wreckage of the Arab-Israeli War; it would reshape borders again. Windows would shatter and widen; windows would narrow and vanish at a single point. Wings break. *How many stories have been lost for the sake of the conflict that would never de-escalate*? Narrowing. Israel — my grandfather, Izzy, as he would be known — would watch his dream actualize as he was dressed as a Turkish soldier, speaking the Turkish of the state, the French of his colonial education, with the memory of the Spanish dialect of Jews of Andalusia — about to become an Israeli.

As soon as he completed his duty and was honorably discharged, he married my grandmother, whom he had met in the Underground Zionist Youth Movement. They had a civil union, a secular Zionist wedding. 1949. Although the law against Zionism had been lifted, there was still a six-month travel ban to the new Israeli state. As soon as this ban was lifted, they boarded a boat, the Anne Marie, and were on the surface of history again, the wide window of ocean, leaving the Bosphorus, into the Aegean, rerouting from a broken pathway, away from a closed border

toward Palestine.

AN
ARROW
A WING

THE FALSE MESSIAHS

Once there was an emperor whose only son fell ill. One physician advised them to spread an acrid salve on a piece of linen and wrap it around the bare body of the patient. Another contradicted him, saying that the boy was too weak to bear the great pain the salve would cause. A third prescribed a sleeping potion, but the fourth feared it might prove injurious to the patient's heart. Then the fifth suggested that they feed the prince a spoonful whenever he woke and was in pain. And so it was done.

When god saw that the soul of Israel had sickened, he wrapped it in the acrid linen of the Exile, and, that the soul might bear the pain, he swathed it in numbing sleep. But lest the sleep destroy the soul, he wakes it from time to time with the hope in a false Messiah, and then pulls it to sleep again until the night will be past and the true Messiah will appear. And for the same reason, even the eyes of sages are sometimes blinded.
—Martin Buber

1912. During the first Balkan War, Salonika, the second largest city in Greece, is taken from the Ottoman Empire by Greek nationalists. Salonika at the time was the largest Jewish majority city in Europe, and a city of Sephardim. 1923. A population transfer between Muslims and Greeks. More than a million Orthodox Christians were sent from what is modern Turkey, and a few hundred thousand Muslims were sent from cities across Greece. This was meant to make permanent the "ethnic" division of Greece & Turkey.

The Jews, however, would stay in Salonika, only to watch as anti-Jewish laws would be passed for the first time in their history.

THEY WILL WAKE US

1941. The Nazis invade Greece, and Salonika is held under military occupation. At the time, 56,000 Jews were living within city limits. During the occupation, nearly 50,000 Jews in Salonika were deported to death camps — most went to Auschwitz. Several hundred Jews holding papers or visas issued by neutral governments — Turkey, Spain, British Mandate Palestine — avoided the camps. Some avoided deportation by escaping into nearby mountains, where they joined partisan groups fighting the Germans.

Fewer than 2,000 Jews survived and returned to Salonika after the war.

Across this narrow border, the Jews in Turkey watched the destruction of Jewish Salonika — many of whom had family there, many of whom were born there.

The border between Turkey and Greece meant life or death.

1943. Nazi forces threaten the outskirts of Istanbul. Yvette's family prepares for an invasion; windows are shuttered; food is rationed.

1945. Nazi forces surrender; Auschwitz is liberated.

The Nazis would never invade Istanbul.

A narrow

1997. In an Italian restaurant in the Bronx, my grandfather turned to me and said, "I'd rather you be smart than be happy." I had just come up from under the table, bored, playing, when he asked, "If I were to give you a second set of eyes, where would you want to put them?"

I said, without hesitation, "In the palms of my hands, so I could open and close them, not be forced to see all the time." He said to me, "What a smart boy! I have such a smart grandson." When we walked together, he held tightly onto my hand, or shoulder, so he wouldn't stumble; he would scan rooms, memorize their limits, count steps, anticipate obstacles, curbs, tables, doors, but always needed someone — gripped my hand hard. He was tall, lumbering, calculating. His Hebrew always sounded like a rebuke, even when it was factual, intellectual, or from what I gathered, tender.

1953. My grandfather began to go blind. He was only 26 years old. It was the year he moved to Jerusalem to take a position in the Israeli foreign ministry. One morning, my grandmother tells me, he woke up and the peripheral vision in his left eye was gone. In the hospital, the doctors couldn't figure out what had happened. There was no visible damage, no history of early blindness in the family, and without an MRI or CT scan — neither of which had been invented at the time — they could only tell that the optic nerve had been damaged, most likely due to an infection. Other than surgery, nothing more could be done.

A narrowing

1959. Izzy wakes up one day to find that the peripheral vision in his right eye has failed. This time it was worse: the vision in the lower rim of his eye recedes as well. He and my grandmother are living in Ethiopia, some of the first Israeli representatives in Africa, with my father and his newborn brother. They had weekly dinners with Haile Selassie, lions roaming unchained in his garden. A year before, emissaries were sent to the south to meet with the Jews in Gondar. When the eye fails suddenly, he is immediately flown to a specialist in Switzerland at the recommendation of a friend. The specialist runs tests for a month, but only comes to the same conclusion: The optic nerve has been damaged; other than surgery, nothing more can be done.

1960. They return to Jerusalem and meet with another doctor, a prominent neurosurgeon. He runs tests, hastily, and makes a similar diagnosis. This time, however, he offers to operate, free of charge. The procedure, a craniotomy, an opening of the skull, was extremely dangerous at the time. The neurosurgeon insisted that it would have to be my grandfather's decision alone. My grandmother tells me now, over the phone, that their friends, other doctors, family members, all said that he shouldn't do the procedure — but my grandfather immediately said yes.

A wing

The surgeon opened his skull, found an infection, cleared it, closed the skull; there was no mishap, no side effect. He said to Izzy: the damage that has been done to your nerve is permanent — irreversible — but what I cleared will slow the infection's inevitable progression. This fear of a complete and final loss of vision hung over his head like the sword of Damocles, my grandmother says to me.

1967. When the Jordanian, Egyptian, and Lebanese armies invaded Israel, all the men on reserves were drafted. My grandfather, who had been on reserve since he arrived in Palestine in 1949, was drafted as well. They had no time to test his sight, so he was stationed, nearly blind, south of Jerusalem, the divided city, in a monastery called Mar Elias. Years later, my father would tell me that when the war ended, after the demilitarized zone wedged at the border of Jordanian and Israeli Jerusalem had been lifted, he made his first contact with Palestinian children his age. In an open field — dusty, unmarked, improvised — two minutes from my father's house, near the King David Hotel, they met to play soccer. As my father tells the story, they played without either Hebrew or Arabic. *What is the name of the language of gestures they used?*

That was the year of the occupation of Sinai, Gaza, West Bank, Golan.

An arrow

When the war ended in 1967, Izzy returned to the Foreign Service, working mostly in France. In those years, few knew how impaired he was. Often he would drive against my grandmother's will. He seemed to not want people to know he was disabled. Or felt that his disability was not a serious obstacle. His own sons were not aware of the extent of it, since he would play bridge with friends, and even, twice, drove to the south of France on his own.

An ing

1974. 47 years old, a year after the Yom Kippur War, my grandfather woke up and discovered that he was completely blind. The field of vision in his left eye had collapsed entirely. On his right eye, his vision narrowed so much that it was merely a pinhole, a tiny focal point that he would peer through for the rest of his life. He was now legally blind; he could no longer drive, could barely read. This time, he couldn't hide the gravity of the situation; he needed someone to walk him everywhere, hold his hand, guide him. Slowly, he was phased out of his work for the state — held on retainer for a few years, since he couldn't do the paperwork anymore — and retired in 1978. This is the version of Israel I know. I met him in this prolonged state: the man who walked slowly, still with a kind of vanity or confidence, and tightly gripped the shoulder or hand of the person nearest him — one of his two sons, my grandmother, my mother, or me when I was younger.

When we walked together, he squeezed my shoulder tightest at every curb. He would scan distances through the pinhole, count small steps, grip hands tighter, trace his fingers on it, memorize it. My grandmother says he would recognize people by touch.

This is where I join him. The damage irreversible. 1975. A cataract formed at the top of his right eye, threatening to cover his vision entirely. Damocles.

He opened a restaurant with a friend he had met in France, a widow. He ran the books, she ran the floor. They called it *Poire et Pomme*. Pear and Apple. For a while it was profitable.

An rr

1972. CT scan invented.
1973. My father drafted into the Israeli Air Force.
1977. MRI invented.
1982. My father serves as a fighter pilot in the first Lebanon war.
1987. Three months after I'm born, my mother and I move to Hatzor air base where my father is working;
        the First Intifada.
2006. Izzy is hospitalized in Tel Aviv, diagnosed with lung cancer,

    the sword falls,
                my father flies to see him;
                                Izzy says he's convinced Israel will lose its soul, is unsustainable;
                                                        he dies; the walls
around the West Bank and Gaza are completed.

2008. My brother is born, given our grandfather's name.
2014. On the phone, my grandmother says to me, *I am no longer obsessed with Israel;*
        Gaza bombarded.

The word *obsessed*.

What is *obsession* if not a synonym for patriotism?

A synonym for family?

Is there a pronoun between I and We?

ITHEYWE IYOUWE IHEWE
ISHEWE IITWE ITHEYWE
        WeTheyI, TheyWeI, IWeThey
          IWETHEY IYOUTHEY IWETHEY

What forms
Between I and They?
In 2014. A hand | a wing over eyes.
Operation Protective Edge.
Rage floods the transpersonal.
A new youth movement forms.
Hand-eye coordination.

A narrowing.

hands tight
but tender
hands slip
from handle
hands | wings
together
pronouns slip
from finger

the song
was not
white not
my hands
obsessed with
holding
light
on my
shoulder

WE THEY I

We read the news.
(a sundered fruit)

It is a hand tearing at leaves.

They are everywhere.
(they are surrounding us)

We I
remember
the words,
Hebrew forms.
שקט. מספיק. די.

They remember.
They forget.
They sleep.

We awaken.
We lose time.
We are lost.

We rush.
We regret.
We fear.

I We
remember him.
His words
echoing. Did they
no longer love
each other?

She refers to herself by her maiden name: Karillo.

(Other loves?
Figures
nameless)

Pear.
Apple.
Habib.
Karillo.
A broken
Mediterranean.

I THEY WE

I left my
Jewishness
for shame of
a broken story.

I return to these
details to understand
what was lost.

How we lost
our pathway back
through the hills
past an old border.

New borders
of mind
preventing
return.

They are us.
We are I.
I am they.
They is I.
I is we.
We is they.

Happiness is
an open
palm
the sun pulsing
at center.

He gripped
his chair
on the balcony
in Ramat Aviv.
He no longer read.
Bats fluttered
in the courtyard.
He listened
to the melody
of Ellington.
He followed it
out of the poem.
And out of his life.

I grip your shoulder.

You grip my shoulder.

We are blind.

The white light

fractures mind.

To tell a story

you must
break a story.

(*the news is a hand tearing at leaves*)

To break a story —
must you

believe in a story

too much?
Or not at all?

Is it to know

some memory

follows us
so far
we wonder
will it follow
our children
and their children?

Or will it
stop
on the imagined border of
this white
page?

Or will it
turn back
toward
the
unmade road

across

uncrossed
borders

mountains
unmet

toward

that temporary heat
that follows us

over centuries?

A FLAG
OF NO
NATION

WALL DRAWING
BOSTON MUSEUM

On a wall surface, any

continuous stretch of wall,

using a hard pencil, place

fifty points at random.

The points should be evenly

distributed over the area

of the wall. All of the

points should be connected

by straight lines.

Sol LeWitt

STUDIES FOR AN EXERCISE IN WORLD CREATION

(OR HOW TO MAKE, OR UNMAKE, A NATION)

—*after Sol LeWitt*

WINDOW [*Breath*]

From a window, any opening,   limit or

edge with a   continuous drop in alt-

itude,   ideally over an area

where many   can see [e.g., busy int-

ersection or   public forum], lower

the flag,   fasten to pole.

Let it be shown   in all weather.

Windstorm, sandstorm, hail.   Witnesses below

are called to attention.   The flag is lifting.

WALL [*Domain*]

On a wall surface,   any unbroken

horizontal plane: stretch the flag. [Fasten

or raise and   hold it up suspend-

ed.]   Let the ambient air

jostle it in   any direction. Witnesses

participate, pull it,   test its elasticity,   release.

Let the flag sit;   imagine passage:

press hard.   Turn away   close eyes

listen to it waver.

LIGHT [*Frame*]

Through the flag,   light   [the activating agent]

falls.   Sight is stimulated.   Witnesses stand

underneath, flag overhead,   walk together

to the nearest source   of light. Brightness

passes through: copper,   turquoise, white.

Witnesses, move closer, meet at   center, make flag

slacken,   pull again til it's taut. Measure how it

changes under

                fluorescence,   tungsten,   fire, sun.

EARTH [*Aftermath*]

Onto the flag, for burial, place soil,   cover.

If soil is unavailable,   any   refuse will do

[any set   of   items of shared substance

that   have been emptied of use]. Fistful on fistful,

alone or with the people near you   (citizens of any

nation), obscure the flag. Make a column,

pyramid, or layer of sediment

over flag's surface   [image of eye opening].   Heap

until flag is   completely concealed.

BODY [*Nauman*]

Against   the flag, press your body

[witnesses   must   hold flag laterally]

Press hard. Feel skin   against flag.

Fall into it, limbs unbent   [imagine pressing

hard]. Witnesses   wrap,   guide

you to the ground. Close eyes   , detect:

gravity, body   against earth,

flag mediating pressure.   Contact.

Stand, shrouded.   Tug at folds, carry further.

AIR [*Nonsense*]

To fill the flag,　　　　any kind of air may be used

　　　　　:　　　　　a witness's breath,

crosswind, headwind, trade wind,　random prayer,

the steady current of an　　　　　industrial fan,

the intentions of ten men and women,

permanent music,　　　　a surveilled scream.

Any action to lift it inside; outside:

the given weather will determine its orientation. Mon-

itor wind's direction, let it move without interference.

DELIVERY

To deliver the flag to any state body or principal polit-

ical figure, wrap it in the body of the kit for dissemi-

nation, this poem enclosed.   Conceal the flag in your

belongings.   Enter airport, enter seaport;   treat your

body as a vessel.   A sequence of similar bodies con-

ceals the flag and forms an unviewable parade: [Imag-

ine our largest organ, iterating]. As it   moves through

worn thresholds, security checks, it is a distress signal,

only to turn into a transitory marker of distance.

ETYMOLOGY

From the root of   the word, vexill-

ology, the study of flags: the Latin

word for skin: *vellum*.   Consider

the concept: *the logic of skin.*   Think of

the flag as   skin.   Imagine

the organs, the body it   conceals, what it

can sense, feel.   Think of a human being's

skin as a flag. Imagine the nation it   represents;

the displaced air it presses against.

FLAG INVENTION I

In 1909, in Istanbul, a student-run organization devel-

oped the Pan-Arab flag, its colors lifted from a   13th-

century poem by Safi al-Din Al-Hilli   (*when sublime*

feelings his heart fill). In 1914, Paris,   the Young Arab

Society designed a new iteration of the flag   (Sharif

Hussein added the color red),   which was adopted in

1916 (Arab Revolt)

1948 (Naqba).

consider   — *sing* —   the dates:

1909, 1914, 1916, 1948, 1967, 2019

FLAG INVENTION II

In 1885, in Rishon LeZion, Fanny Abramovitch and

Israel Belkind designed the Flag of Judah   (*bring*

witness the swords, did we lose hope)   as a marker

of a new settlement. In 1897,   Switzerland,

Morris Harris, a New Yorker,   presented a de-

sign for the flag of a new state, which was adopted in

                        1898 (Second Zionist Congress)

                        1948 (War of Independence).

consider   — *sing* —   these dates:

          1885, 1897, 1898, 1948, 1967, 2019

NATIONAL SONG

During the final note of national song, which is the

longest, begin to disassemble the machinery of citi-

zenship. Or if the song is just beginning, but is

held in fermata, begin screaming. The *gestureless sa-*

lute may be used: no arms raised, never facing the

flag, only your neighbor, mouth closed. As soon as

patriotic effect is desired, incinerate the flag. Use its

ash to paint lines of flight. Foxtails are burning. The

buildings are swept aside like wheat. *Salute*: repeat.

OCEAN

Beneath the ocean, the divine body, the deflection of a

sequence of forms, marching into the unending   or-

dering of. One pole projecting into sky.   Another

deeper into ocean. The ocean of obstructions.   The

charge on the individual. The charge on many: on

those bodies who bend the perimeter of other bodies.

Watch the flag through optical obstructions (your be-

droom window, school window, stained glass,   LCD

[ion-strengthened   glass, antinomy, boron], ice).

BENT FLAGPOLE

In a domain   in which a wall of light diffuses our

attention, there is a flagpole. The flagpole has the flag

of a nation on it. It is not necessarily a nation that you

recognize [the necessary action]. Pick up the flag,

briskly lower it, raise it,   ceremoniously lower it,

remove it. Rush into the wall of light. Tomorrow, you

may begin by breathing.   You may begin

by wondering   what kind of projection this pole is,

what kind of wall may be passed through,   perceived.

OTHER FLAGS

Before the aftermath, during hours of darkness,   the

flag must be fully illuminated.   Remain silent; it will

be seen. Ordinarily, the flag should be displayed in the

sun. Cyclones, war, siege, electrical fire may remove it.

No superior prominence than when it seeks no honor.

Other flags raised nearby must stand.   The palm, syn-

tagm. In a time of peace; in a time of internationalism.

The flag: the bright bits of flame   in a long se-

quence of bodies, the durational hum of passing eras.

OF

Of it, if, from about behind the of now for, for the under through. Into, off, belonged to, to the flag. Over over over, the within of into first. The widened-from, the fear of into Domain, child, out of, out of leisure, across love; when the exquisite becomes expedient the revolution has begun.

Begin each action with a preposition: "Where to?" she asks. Home or out. From home, back home, or into

the world?

THE

These are the strong words that carry more weight

than words, this is the game that we established when

we were young. The ocean was the great skin. The

ocean laughed while we were asking. The body, the

earth, the white night, never woken to. We called our

nation: birth.

Behind each preposition: the situation at hand. Our

hand toward, for, the mouth of a larger morning:

night, unclosed.

FOR LETTING

For letting go of the flag, *for* beneath and coming up

of the flag, *for* the asking price of the flag, *for* the true

knowledge of the flag, *for* the falling order of the flag's

release, *for* the leaves that fall near the flag, *for*

emotion behind surface of loss, *for* counting, *for* the

long list of lost names, *for* the true release of the flag,

for the ashes that swarm into marches of the true seas,

for releasing into natural language the commanding

voice, *for* the computational force, *for* the

GO OF

Strict list of last troubles, *for* the terror of the moon

that pulls us in this still war, *for* the noose of identity,

for the war on the word on the word on the word,

for the son who engendered bad news, *for* how we

told our only son that this is the war on the word &

how we told our only remaining daughter that this is

a war on the word, *for* the pause that is true breath,

for the pause that is false breath concealing hurrying

thoughts: those that race til exhalation: total.

CAVE I [DIRECTIVE]

Into the poem, stillness. *Against* initial action, mute

force. Enter word into poem, situate under

title. Let it file along the span of nine lines. Martyr.

The cave that is filled with language. The cave whose

content is noise. The cave whose content is silence,

noisy earth churning beneath it: particles of grammar,

tornado. Weather unheard of. Not known before we

had begun talking. The cave caves, and silence silences

the tall. The bell that falls that hears the age.

CAVE II [CONSECUTIVE]

At the start of the consecutive song, the breaking

of voice, thought turning to stone. Thought thrown.

Thought the night that covers vengeful sleep. What is

witnessed. At the start of the consecutive song: digits

of an outward catastrophe. One that resists its com-

plete cause. At the start of the consecutive song:

passion spent. How were your words used when

the pomegranates fell? How were your words taken

[felt] when the oranges stopped falling?

CAVE III
For Yael Bartana

Into Cave III, voice turned voidward.   To un-void.

To turn tender noun to wall of proper nouns. Yvette

pours us coffee. When she was in Mersin, she was cut

off from parents. Envious of sister. New to the

world. Tilt this phone, this plane, this city. The air is

medium, the friction from which voice

forms. This is the song of dreamlessness. Momentary

limb, heave us into the home of having

known what to be called. To let the air speak.

CAVE IV [1982]

As the air carves the flag, flag carves the air.

My father learned to make his way in a desert.

A desert is a flattened cave. Like a cardboard

box, taken apart, the desert is. Creates no shadow.

Is completely exposed. We walked across it,

figuring the dirt, figuring those who had brought

us here. The scene is flat. The scene has no depth,

no cave. We lift it inside, inside the song that encloses

the song of collapse. We carry the cave in our arms.

CAVE V
For David Hammons

When the flag covers your head. When it rests on your

vision. When strange night turns into lawful day.

The flag is torn from itself. The flag announces

your name. A flag is pulled from the flag.

What is pulled stands between man

and man, sight and sight. When perception falls

through. Take this sight, into the heart of. Those fruits

that have fallen [pomegranate, orange]. They will lie

on the ground, ripe, for as long as we need them to.

CAVE VI [1992]

As a cave falls behind you, shadow, its contents not

disclosed, but rather, turquoise, touches the surface

of song. Together, we lift the corners of the light.

The light is tugged taut at its four corners. A roof

forms over our history, and that which is unwritten.

Now we can witness unending space. Lift the corners

of light higher. Let the air stir it. Lift the corners of

earth. Lift the corners of body. Higher. Under the

banner of darkness, we share new light. We practice.

HAMSA
FLAG

from: Yvette Haviv <yvehav@gmail.com> date: Wed, Aug 8, 2012 at 3:49 AM to: Tom Haviv <tmhaviv@gmail.com>

YVETTE | TOM

Tom,
my beloved grandson,
your mail touched
a sensitive vein in me.

This is my humble prayer:

If all the deep,
primary longing
for peace
inherent
to every human being
was assembled
uniting, connecting us
with the universe,
wouldn't thus
come out
a godly strength able
to overcome fear, greed, vanity, violence,
opening our
eyes to see at last the
eyes of the other living creatures,
discovering the essence "being"?

Is the peace dream an "illusion"?
I pray and pray
with all the strength left
in me that this "illusion"
comes alive, for the sake of
my children, grandchildren,
for the sake of
generations to come.
Amen.

Love, grandma

להתגבר על פחד, חמדנות, יהירות, אלימות

to overcome fear, greed, vanity, violence

للتغلب على الخوف والجشع والغرور والعنف

ON THE HAMSA FLAG

I first imagined the Hamsa Flag in 2009 while reading an essay in the *New York Times* about a proposed one-state solution in Israel|Palestine. Up until then, I had only known of the two-state solution, and had abided by the idea that it was integral to the "peace process." As soon as I finished the article, I remember having an immediate, almost visceral response: For such a utopia to exist, the flags of both sides would have to be abandoned, and a new flag introduced. I was struck by what I saw as a design flaw intrinsic to the conflict. The design of the flags themselves, distinctly representing both peoples' states and claims, was blocking our political imagination and forming yet another obstacle in the path toward civil rights, justice, and peace.

At its root, it was a simple thought. I felt that most Israelis would never agree to live under the Pan-Arab colors of the Palestinian flag and most Palestinians would never agree to live under the blue and white — the Magen David — of the Israeli flag.

As soon as the thought came, the symbol followed: the hamsa. It was instinctive, intuitive, and absolutely clear: This was the natural symbol of the merging of two peoples. *The open palm*.

Why this symbol? Jews, Muslims, and Christians, Arabs, Turks, and Kurds, and people in the Balkans and across North Africa have all been wearing the hamsa in some form as a spiritual emblem for hundreds, if not thousands, of years. It was a symbol that naturally bypassed otherwise sharp, or deadly, borders of history, culture, and identity; in its simplicity, in its familiarity and otherworldliness, it seemed to have the power to unify, to create surprising kinships.

I felt a flag was necessary because a movement would be necessary, because there need to be flags of peace and resistance, flags of the imagination, flags that can say things we cannot yet articulate in words. The flag was not designed as a reaction, or to be entangled in the dialectic of Jew and non-Jew. It was designed with the hope of challenging and ultimately dismantling the violent binaries that underlie the crisis in Israel|Palestine — and to set the stage for something new. *The world to come*.

ON THE DESIGN

The colors of the flag, turquoise and copper, together signify activation. Copper (Cu) is the element that, once oxidized in water, creates the compound turquoise. Therefore, copper is the source of the activated potential that is turquoise. Taking this further as metaphor, the copper and turquoise flag suggests the potential for political, spiritual, and communal activation inherent within each one of us. Thus the flag's image reveals an elemental, latent copper resting on the backdrop of an activated turquoise expanse.

In some craft traditions, a turquoise stone is used as an eye at the center of the palm of the hamsa. In the case of this flag, the turquoise eye has been expanded and abstracted into the all-embracing background, creating an ocean or horizon of activated turquoise behind the open palm. The hamsa in this formation is designed to represent a vast, shifting, hybrid community of many tribes (and beyond the very notion of tribe), of many nations (and beyond the very notion of nation), all emerging from a common elemental source.

The hamsa is an apotropaic symbol; a symbol that redirects energy (from the Greek *apo*, meaning away, and *tropos*, meaning turn). The talisman is typically used to protect its wearer from the evil eye; the hamsa in its new formation — on a flag — intends to serve as a collective ward against evil.

FLAG AS QUESTION

The meaning and impact of the Hamsa Flag project continues to be shaped by and for community; it has been used, studied, critiqued, and informed by many collaborators and organizations.

As it is used, the flag raises more questions that require ever-new voices and perspectives.

What form should the flag take?
What place or no-place should it represent?
Who will raise and fly it?
What causes will it represent?
A binational state?
A federation of Middle Eastern states?
A flag against nationalism?
A flag of a renewed internationalist movement?
A flag of Palestinian solidarity?
A flag of Mizrahi & Sephardi solidarity?
A flag of Jewish & Muslim solidarity?
A flag of the Levant?
A flag of the Mediterranean?
Is it a flag of peace?
Is it a flag of resistance?
Can it be both?

I meet you here, inviting you to imagine this with me.

FLAG REFER ENCES

IMAGES

Unless otherwise noted, photos by Tom Haviv or from his family archive

ABOUT TOM HAVIV

Tom Haviv is a writer, multimedia artist, and organizer based in Brooklyn and born in Israel.
A Flag of No Nation is his debut book of poetry. He is the creator of the Hamsa Flag, a project designed to stimulate conversation about the future of Israel|Palestine, Mizrahi/Sephardi culture, and Jewish/Muslim solidarity. Tom is also the cofounder of Ayin Press and the author of two children's books, *Woven* and *The Porcupine Prince*.

ABOUT YVETTE HAVIV

An idealist, multilinguist, and painter, Yvette Haviv (née Karillo) was born in 1928 in Istanbul, Turkey. She is the granddaughter of a rabbi of a Portuguese synagogue in Odessa. A Pisces, she was educated in Notre Dame de Sion school in Istanbul, where, as the top student of her class in 1936, she was asked to deliver flowers to Mustafa Kemal Atatürk. At the time, a progressive nun in her school, Mère Emmanuelle, encouraged her to pursue her Jewishness against the backdrop of World War II and the Shoah. At 15, she joined the underground Zionist movement, and soon after married Israel "Izzy" Haviv and moved to Israel.

She and her husband worked in the foreign service for many years, serving in Ethiopia, Romania, and France. She also worked as a speechwriter for four Israeli presidents. In 1978, she got her master's degree in art history from Tel Aviv University and began to paint with oils and acrylics. A Peace Now activist in the '80s and '90s, she was awarded a presidential medal for her service. After her husband passed away, she moved to Herzliya, then went to live with her sister in Virginia, and later joined her son and grandson in a small town near Toledo, Ohio. She passed away in May 2019.

ACKNOWLEDGMENTS

Thank you to Yvette Haviv, Israel Haviv, Shlomo Haviv, Sharon Haviv, Lucy Andersen, Ari Bloomekatz, Maia Ipp, Arielle Angel, Jacob Plitman, Madeleine Tarrou, Eden Pearlstein, Naomi Dann, Robin Margolis, Ben Ratskoff, Max Berger, the Mizrahi/Sephardi Caucus of JFREJ, Joanna Steinhardt, Penina Eilberg-Schwartz, Ayin Press, Aviva Bogart, Julie Agoos, Ben Lerner, Anselm Berrigan, Marjorie Welish, Devin Naar, James Loop, Connie Mae Concepción Oliver, Hannah Roodman, Liane Al-Ghusain, Gabrielle Spear, Stacy Skolnik, Hannah Buonaguro, Irene Siegel, Hamid Ouali, Jon Levin, Samantha Fine, Jessie Kritt, and Lawrence Sanfilippo.

Some poems have appeared in *Fence, Conjunctions, Black Sun Lit, PROTOCOLS, Unruly Blog,* and elsewhere.

MY EYES

after the white sky
after the white ocean
the eyeless children
went toward
new loves

the islands were love and love lost
paradise was a broken heart
horizon was a canvas again

after white
ocean there
were many lovers
the loves were each finger
a finger pointing
a finger not pointing
a finger touching firmly
the full tenderness of unknowing
bled into the hard angle
of my new eye

my new eye
sorted into
a sea of us
should we ever
face crisis (again)
or as the ocean is a friend
— a first friend
so it pearled from the branches
of my broken sight: new eyes

i took one of them
no ships would be built
and placed my new eye
the color of ocean,
earth, and bleeding
star-yellow
fruit
and looked farther
to a land of
unlearned homes
names built
in the century before
the word

*

i knew this place without moving

*

the branch pearled more eyes
for you and me and all the loves to be